I Actually Wore This

Clothes We Can't Believe We Bought

...lly Wore This

Clothes We Can't Believe We Bought

Written by Tom Coleman
Photography by Jerome Jakubiec

RIZZOLI
NEW YORK

New York · Paris · London · Milan

To my mom, Joan Coleman, a lady of great style and impeccable timing

— Tom Coleman

To Annie DeWitt, who graces my life with daily multiple wardrobe changes

— Jerome Jakubiec

Contents

Introduction

A lot of fashion books will tell you exactly what to wear for brunch in Barbuda or offer a lengthy treatise on the history of the espadrille. Fashion books are also very good at coming up with rules you should never break—no open-toed shoes while eating an open-faced sandwich!—and make it very clear that fashion is serious business. And, if you don't think it is serious business, maybe you should rewatch that scene in *The Devil Wears Prada*, where Meryl Streep rips poor Anne Hathaway a new one over a blue sweater. I'm still shaking.

I Actually Wore This is not that kind of book. It never preaches. It never judges. It never suggests you might become a better person by wearing Egyptian cotton. In fact, it celebrates those times when taste takes a holiday—the times when you bought an article of clothing that would later give you a case of the jerks. The jerks isn't merely when you feel like a jerk but a condition when your body involuntarily jerks upon remembering something embarrassing you did. *I Actually Wore This* embraces those cringe-inducing garments, those items that will forever cause you to mutter, "What was I thinking?" when you see them hanging in your closet. Bedazzled tube tops, a Speedo the size of a cocktail napkin, and Navajo-blanket ponchos, this is your safe space.

Jerome and I would like to hugely thank the normally stylish people who participated in this book. They were kind and brave enough to dig through their closets and find their most regrettable clothing item, allow themselves to be photographed wearing it, and tell their stories. The people in this book are a wide range of accomplished and rational humans, illustrating that a momentary lapse in fashion judgment can affect anyone. *Bad clothes can happen to good people*: the T-shirts are at the printers.

While working on the book, some common themes arose in terms of why and how the regrettable items ended up in people's closets. Sample sales were the culprit more than once, as it seems people are willing to buy Misfit-Toy fashion if it's drastically reduced and slapped with the name of a designer they recognize. "Who knows, I might wear a Chanel gas mask someday." Vintage boutiques, resale shops, and secondhand stores, no matter what you call them, they too supplied a handful of items for our pantheon of regrettable garments. This proves that bad taste, much like the German measles, needs to be eradicated quickly so that it cannot spread to future generations.

I'd be remiss if I didn't offer my own story of a glaring fashion faux pas. My item in question is a tweed vest I purchased in my twenties from a tiny ad in the back of *The New Yorker*. Nestled between ads for pure Vermont maple syrup and guided tours of the Galapagos was an ad for 100-percent-authentic Scottish tweed vests. The ad featured a clip-art photo of a guy who looked like a very distant cousin of Sean Connery wearing a tweed vest, smoking a pipe, and holding a border collie on a leash. Sold! I knew that once the vest arrived in the mail, my life would change. Soon I'd be invited for weekend shooting parties at Balmoral and have clever friends named Cecil and Bryony.

When the vest arrived, it was very nice tweed. It also had genuine horn buttons. The surprise came when I tried it on. The top button was about three inches from my chin, and the shoulders were cut very square. It fit me like a fancy life preserver. It was fashioned from very thick and heavy tweed, making it impossible to wear under a jacket. The couple of times I did wear it, I looked like a waiter at an *Oliver Twist*–themed restaurant: "Come in before eight for all-you-can-eat gruel at "Twisties!" I retired the vest soon after and forgot about it until a few years ago, when my sister called asking about it. "Do you still have that tweed vest?" she said. Maybe I had been wrong about the vest after all? If someone remembered it, then it must have made a strong impression. "Yeah, I still have it," I said, already envisioning myself wearing it again. "Great," she said. "Can I borrow it? One of the kids is going as Pinocchio for Halloween."

Jerk.

Tom Coleman

Jean-Michel Placent *Private art advisor, New York City*

REGRETTABLE ARTICLE OF CLOTHING: Versace shirt

PURCHASED: New York City, in 1992, for approximately $500

TIMES WORN: 2

That Bush guy—the first one—was in the White House. "I'm Too Sexy" was number one and I felt a need to own a shirt with a very large American Indian on the front. OK, correction, Native American. And since we're being correct here, anything billowy, silk, and Versace probably shouldn't be called a shirt. That thing I bought was pretty much a blouse.

I bought the shirt to wear to the opening-night gala at the Metropolitan Opera. I was new in the city and thought it would set me apart from everyone else in a tuxedo. Believe me, when you wear a shirt that makes you look like you're part of some Navajo-themed Cirque du Soleil production, you definitely set yourself apart. More than a few people assumed I was part of the evening's entertainment, perhaps a fire-eater or ropewalker. One woman said she was offended by the shirt, something to do with how the pony on the sleeve was being treated.

After the gala, I banished the shirt to the back of my closet and tried to forget about it. Then I brought it out on Halloween a couple of years ago. I wore it with a pair of Girbaud jeans and Rollerblades. I went as the '90s.

9

It was pretty much a blouse.

Molly Shannon *Actress, Los Angeles*

REGRETTABLE ARTICLE OF CLOTHING: Flowered jumpsuit

PURCHASED: Banana Republic, in Boston, in 2014, for $120

TIMES WORN: Almost 1

A moms' getaway weekend was planned with my friend Martel at a fancy ranch in Carmel, so I thought I'd buy something new. I wasn't sure what to wear to a moms' weekend, but I wanted to look really sharp. I wanted it to be like a Nancy Meyer movie, where I'd walk down the stairs in my new outfit and make a grand entrance. Then I'd drink chardonnay with the ladies and we'd all throw our heads back and laugh.

I debated a few different looks before deciding on the jumpsuit. A denim shirt-and-prairie skirt combo was considered and rejected, as was a vintage sundress covered in daisies. For some reason, the jumpsuit spoke to me.

The first night we arrived at the ranch, Martel and I were having cocktails upstairs as we got ready to go down to dinner. Martel is from Alabama and has a very heavy Southern accent—that fact is crucial to the story. I was wearing the jumpsuit, convinced I had really nailed it, and was waiting for Martel to comment. Martel took a sip of her drink, looked at me, and said, "My, you look very resoooooort." The word *resort* took her about five seconds to say with her accent, and by the time she had finished drawling it out, I knew I had made a horrible mistake. I quickly changed into something else.

Women named Martel know things. They just do.

Angela Dimayuga *Executive chef at Mission Chinese, New York City*

REGRETTABLE ARTICLE OF CLOTHING: Pantsuit

PURCHASED: New York City, in 2013, for $200

TIMES WORN: 1

Once a year, my friends and I have a weekend where we all go away together. The destination changes, but one thing remains constant—each of us must bring a ridiculous outfit that we change into at some point during the weekend. The goal is to surprise everyone. One minute you're sitting there drinking a glass of wine in a T-shirt and jeans, and then you go into the bathroom and emerge in a rhinestone evening gown. We realize there's a weird, wacky British country house-party vibe to the whole thing, but we like that.

I bought the pantsuit specifically for this weekend. It is two pieces and something I thought Megan Draper would buy with some of that divorce money. I practiced putting it on quickly so I could maximize the element of surprise. I had gotten my time down to under ten seconds. Yes, a grown woman with a job and everything was doing this.

12

I waited for just the right moment. I had put the pantsuit in a bag in a hall closet. When someone suggested we open another bottle of wine, I quickly volunteered and sprang into action. I grabbed the bag, went into the kitchen, and changed behind the open refrigerator door in case anyone came in. I think I broke my own time record. When I rejoined the others with the wine in hand, I got a standing ovation.

It was something I thought Megan Draper would buy with some of that divorce money.

Chip Kidd *Book-cover designer/coauthor of* True Prep, *New York City*

REGRETTABLE ARTICLE OF CLOTHING: Rugby shirt

PURCHASED: Boston, in 2009, for approximately $250

TIMES WORN: 6

Before I wore this shirt, I never knew there were so many ways you could interpret the phrase "Nice shirt." Some people, usually cops and young moms, would be sincere and offer a compliment when they said it. But the packs of teens who would sneer and mumble it under their breath as they passed me on the street, they used it as a weapon. I wanted to scream back, "Really? Well, nice hair, One Direction!" But I knew that would end with me wearing zip-tie handcuffs in the back of a patrol car.

"Did you notice how well it's made?" I found myself saying a lot when I wore the shirt. I thought if I could show people the detailed stitching, finished seams, and genuine horn buttons, they would understand and appreciate the shirt. That way, I was hoping they would view me as sartorially savvy versus ass clown.

I originally bought the shirt for a sailing trip to Maine with friends. When I arrived, I quickly learned that real sailors wear faded Phish T-shirts and old Patagonia shorts covered in linseed oil, not shirts that make you look like you're in the chorus of *Godspell*. I found this out about ten minutes after I arrived. Two twelve-year-olds were helping me with my luggage. As I walked away, they both muttered, "Nice shirt." I'm pretty sure neither of them were cops.

Claire Distenfeld *Owner, Fivestory boutique, New York City*

REGRETTABLE ARTICLE OF CLOTHING: Comme des Garçons dress

PURCHASED: New York City, in 2012, for $475

TIMES WORN: 1

I had broken up with my boyfriend and sat around brooding long enough. I decided it was time to get back out there. I was going to make a fresh start and meet new people. The question was, What should this new me wear?

I found this Comme des Garçons dress in a vintage shop. It wasn't really me, but since I was the new me, maybe it was. It was sheer on top with two strategically placed sunbursts. If I wanted to meet new people, this should do it.

A couple of nights later, I met friends at a bar and wore the dress. The dress and the new me were having a good time. I was back! A male hand tapped me on the shoulder, and from the smiles of my friends, I sensed it was attached to someone good. I realize this is the part of the story where it should turn out to be Johnny Depp and we run off to that island he owns, but it was actually my ex-boyfriend. We hadn't seen each other in awhile, and after a few jokes about the dress, we sat and talked. By the end of the night, we were back together.

As for the epilogue of this tale, the dress is now officially retired, and my boyfriend is now my husband. Good work, sunbursts.

If I wanted to meet new people, this should do it.

Matt Hanna *Head of original programming at Esquire Network, Los Angeles*

REGRETTABLE ARTICLE OF CLOTHING: Alexander McQueen coat

PURCHASED: New York City, in 2010, for $500

TIMES WORN: 1

When I saw this coat on the rack at the Alexander McQueen sample sale, I thought I had really scored. A well-tailored black cashmere coat for $500... sold! However, I was in for a little surprise. On the back of the coat was a port-hole, or a slice, or a gaping wound—I'm not exactly sure what to call it. But yes, the back of the coat had a foot-long section where the fabric was intentionally cut, leaving it wide open to flap in the wind.

I have no idea as to the thinking behind this bizarre design element. It was possibly so you could see what someone was wearing under the coat, or maybe it was just to screw with the minds of guys who thought they were getting a great deal at a sample sale. The rest of the coat was beautiful, so I decided I could figure out how to deal with this one little flaw and bought it anyway.

When I took the coat home and modeled it for my wife, she loved it. Then I turned around, and she was even more confused than I was. "Huh, what, why, explain?" were the words she finally managed to utter as she surveyed my coat of gaping cashmere. I convinced her I had a plan and that soon the coat would be healed.

I took the coat to my tailor. He's a man of few words, and after he examined it, I knew from three shakes of his head that it could not be saved. He explained that there wasn't enough fabric to simply sew up the hole, as it would pucker and destroy the fit. It was at that moment I realized I would have to face the truth and let the coat go peacefully.

Roz Chast *Cartoonist/author of* Can't We Talk About Something
More Pleasant?, *Connecticut and New York City*

REGRETTABLE ARTICLE OF CLOTHING: Terrible shirt

PURCHASED: Repressed

TIMES WORN: Deeply repressed

_____

22

Repressed.

John Mulaney *Comedian, Los Angeles*

REGRETTABLE ARTICLE OF CLOTHING: T-shirt

PURCHASED: Gift, 2013

TIMES WORN: 3

I'm not much of a risk-taker when it comes to fashion. I dress a lot like the history teacher that everyone likes, even though he's a tough grader.

I did a sketch on *Kroll Show* with Nick Kroll called "Too Much Tuna." The sketch would later be the inspiration for our Broadway show "Oh Hello," which is about two old guys from the Upper West Side named Gil and George who love Alan Alda, Steely Dan, and light jazz. We asked the wardrobe department to make an XXL T-shirt for my character to wear over a turtleneck that said *Jazz Forever*. We wanted it to look like something you'd buy on the way out of a jazz-fusion concert at the Beacon Theatre. It came out great.

I liked the shirt so much, I asked the nice wardrobe people to make me one in my size. They made me two, in case there was ever a T-shirt accident.

If and when I become an old guy on the Upper West Side, I shall wear my shirt proudly as I sit on a park bench, doing the Sunday *New York Times* crossword in *pen*.

Leandra Medine *Writer/founder of Man Repeller, New York City*

REGRETTABLE ARTICLE OF CLOTHING: Yohji Yamamoto jacket

PURCHASED: Bergdorf Goodman, in May 2012, for $2,700

TIMES WORN: 3

The jacket is amazing, and I don't regret owning it. The only thing I regret is that it was rather pricey. I think if you amortized the cost of the jacket over the number of times I've worn it, you'd come to a figure that is close to my entire operating budget during four years of college. Believe me, that jacket is a whole lot of ramen.

I originally bought the jacket to wear at my wedding, so I thought I was allowed something a little spendy. Other brides want a thousand doves released or to ride in a Cinderella carriage. Me, I wanted a Yohji Yamamoto jacket.

The jacket is like a work of art, so it's hard to pull off as an everyday piece. Maybe if you were Björk or St. Vincent you could wear it every day, but for a working girl who is constantly in and out of cabs and subways, it's not the most practical thing to wear.

I didn't end up wearing the jacket at my wedding after all. I decided to go with a custom-made white motorcycle jacket instead—you know, something more traditional. If we ever decide to renew our vows, maybe I'll wear the jacket. Because you know the old adage, "something borrowed, something blue, something Yamamoto."

Believe me, this jacket is a whole lot of ramen.

Aaron Fox *Tennis pro, Los Angeles*

REGRETTABLE ARTICLE OF CLOTHING: Camouflage shirt

PURCHASED: New York City, in 2009, for $30

TIMES WORN: 5

This shirt has lived a couple of lives. I bought it at an army surplus store in New York City during a brief period in 2009 when camouflage was cool. It seems that every couple of years, camouflage gets cool for ten minutes and you see it everywhere. Then somebody declares it's no longer cool, and all the camouflage goes back into hiding, which I guess it's good at.

When I first bought this shirt, I wore it really wrinkled right out of the dryer. It never became one of my favorites, so eventually it got pushed to the back of the closet.

One day I needed a project, so I decided to clean my closet. For some reason, when I came upon the camouflage shirt, I decided to cut off its sleeves. I'm not exactly sure why, although someone may have been watching a lot of *Project Runway* at the time. I didn't do a very good job, as one of the armholes is somewhat larger than the other.

I think the only time Camo Shirt 2.0 made it out in public was as part of a last-minute G.I. Joe Halloween costume. I remember it was cold that night, and I really wished I had sleeves.

28

Lee Potter *Art dealer, New York City*

REGRETTABLE ARTICLE OF CLOTHING: Cocktail dress

PURCHASED: Bergdorf Goodman, in 2005, for $1,500

TIMES WORN: 2

Orange works great for Cheetos, traffic cones, and Mario Batali's Crocs. But I've learned that it's not the easiest color to pull off on a dress unless you're Sofia Vergara or a Real Housewife of Cartagena.

I bought the dress to wear to a black-tie party. Normally I would wear black, but for some reason, I decided I wanted to set myself apart from the pack. No polite little black dress for me—I was going to wear a color. I know, I'm such a rebel.

Nobody made any direct comments about the dress, but people did keep asking me if I had been somewhere before the party or if I was going somewhere after. I took that to mean they were looking for an explanation: Had I been at Carrot Top's birthday party, or was I headed to a Halloween-themed wedding?

Van Gogh supposedly said that orange is the color of madness. In the case of this dress, I'll just plead a little temporary insanity.

I decided I wanted to set myself apart from the pack.

DeVinn Bruce *Creative director, New York City*

REGRETTABLE ARTICLE OF CLOTHING: Issey Miyake trench coat

PURCHASED: Barneys New York, 1970-ish, for $800

TIMES WORN: 2

I'm not usually an alarmist, but I think this coat tried to kill me.

The coat was my first big purchase after I got a real job. I bought it at Barneys and remember feeling like such an adult walking down the street with my coat in the cool black Barneys shopping bag.

The coat was by Issey Miyake, the designer famous for making heavily pleated clothing and all of Steve Jobs's black turtlenecks. (Fun fact!) He takes risks with his designs, as evidenced by my coat, which resembled a flying squirrel in full extension.

I wore the coat for the first time to a party downtown. I couldn't wait to get there and make an entrance in my new coat. However, I made more of an entrance when I went to enter the subway, stepped on the giant coat's hem, tripped myself, and tumbled down the stairs. I wasn't injured—just a bit rattled—and decided that sometimes being fashionable comes at a cost.

I had a nice time at the party and got some compliments on my coat. I was happy as I headed home uptown, as my return trip on the subway was without incident. Or so I thought.

Subway doors open on both sides, and you're never really sure on which side the doors will open. It's a fun little guessing game New Yorkers play. That night, I was standing with my back against one door and when the subway came to my stop, I attempted to exit through the door across from me. But, there was a slight problem. My coat was stuck in the door behind me and when I went to walk across the car, I was quickly snapped back in place like a cheap slingshot. If I pulled the coat I'd tear it, so I would have to wait till the next stop when the door would open and release the coat. Thanks to my coat, I was now on my way to Harlem at two a.m.

Is it possible to get a restraining order against a coat?

My coat resembled a flying squirrel in full extension.

Susan Sandlund *Psychologist, Katonah, New York*

REGRETTABLE ARTICLE OF CLOTHING: Cocktail dress

PURCHASED: Neiman Marcus in Washington, D.C., in 1988, for $300

TIMES WORN: 1

There's a lot going on with this dress. On first glance, it appears to be just a random animal print, but if you look closely, you'll see not one but several animal prints. There's cheetah, giraffe, leopard, and maybe a little zebra all living together in harmony. Whoever designed the fabric went a little Doctor Moreau and decided to throw together a bunch of different patterns from nature and see what happened. This dress happened.

I was a little unsure of the dress from the start. I bought it at Neiman Marcus—on sale—so I managed to convince myself that it must be good. Neiman Marcus doesn't sell crap, right? Neiman Marcus sells gold-plated teddy bears and helicopter rides over the pyramids. People love Neiman Marcus!

I wore the dress to a black-tie event. The zipper broke early in the evening, so I remember spending a lot of time in the bathroom begging for safety pins. I used one of those miniscule safety pins you find in travel-sized sewing kits, but it lasted about five minutes. I eventually found a larger pin that worked much better, but I was forced to limit my movement for the rest of the evening. Dancing, laughing, and basically enjoying myself were out of the question. I stood with my back against a wall nodding politely through several conversations. Luckily, I was in Washington, D.C., where that's all it takes for people to think you're having a really great time.

Stella Chestnut *Student, Los Angeles*

REGRETTABLE ARTICLE OF CLOTHING: Striped shirt

PURCHASED: Los Angeles, in 2014, for $25

TIMES WORN: 20

I used to wear this shirt all the time—it was one of my favorites. I remember I was excited to wear it to school the day after I got it. I also wore it to a friend's birthday party and to play at a neighbor's house.

Then one day, I just didn't like it anymore. I don't know why, I just didn't. I put it at the bottom of my drawer and didn't want to see it anymore. I didn't have a bad time or anything when I wore the shirt, but it just didn't seem like the same shirt when I looked at it. I can't really explain it, but maybe not everything has a reason behind it. People always think that everything has a reason. I'm not so sure that's true.

Drew Villani *Art director/designer, New York City*

REGRETTABLE ARTICLE OF CLOTHING: Lanvin shirt

PURCHASED: Lanvin in New York City, in 2012, for $350

TIMES WORN: 2

Sometimes there's one little thing that can ruin a piece of clothing. In the case of this shirt, there were two: my nipples.

I'm a huge fan of Lanvin, and if I ever see it at a discount, I jump on it. So when I saw this shirt on sale at a huge markdown, I bought it. I was surprised it was on sale, as most designers never seem to discount the more practical pieces. It's usually the novelty items that are hard to wear, like neon-colored jumpers or jackets with giant squirrels on the back, that go on sale. A black shirt seemed like something I could get a lot of wear out of, and I felt like I had really found a great bargain.

I didn't try on the shirt in the shop, and I only took it out of the bag and removed all those tiny annoying pins on the night I decided to wear it for the first time. I was psyched when I put it on, as it fit me perfectly. When I looked in the mirror, though, I got a little Lanvin surprise: the shirt was bloody see-through!

I'm not a terribly modest person, but wearing a shirt where people can instantly see every inch of you was a bit disconcerting. It wasn't just a little see-through, either; in the right light, it was absolutely transparent. No mystery here—everything was up for inspection. Whether I had an innie or an outie or a mild case of bacne, all would be revealed.

I once had a boss who always said you should never buy anything on sale because things that go on sale are things that nobody wants. What he meant by that is now all too clear—or should I say see-through.

39

When I got home I got a little Lanvin surprise: the shirt was bloody see-through.

Annie DeWitt *Writer, Catskills, New York*

REGRETTABLE ARTICLE OF CLOTHING: Sweater

PURCHASED: Paris, in 2012, €40

TIMES WORN: 2

I was visiting Paris and found this sweater at a flea market in Montmartre. When I saw it, I started to envision where I might wear it. I pictured myself living in a garret in Le Marais, teaching art to fashionable young Parisians, and listening to a lot of Nina Simone. I would throw on this sweater when I strolled down to my local *tabac* to buy another pack of Gauloises. Odd considering I don't smoke, but apparently I did in my fantasy.

The sweater came back home with me to the States. I still loved it, but it didn't fit under any of my coats, so it had to be absolutely perfect sweater weather for me to wear it. That gave me about two days in October when I could rock it.

Over time, the sweater has become my go-to house robe. It's comfortable and roomy, and if someone stops by, it doesn't look like I've been in my robe all day. It's also a big hit with my cats. I think my imaginary French art students would be happy I've kept it.

Fred Spencer *Soccer agent, New York City and London*

REGRETTABLE ARTICLE OF CLOTHING: Button-down patchwork shirt

PURCHASED: Ralph Lauren online in 2014, for $145

TIMES WORN: 2

When you order something online, you always wonder what the postage stamp-sized photo you click on will actually look like when it shows up at your door. In the case of this shirt, the real thing exceeded my expectations, but I'm not sure that's a good thing.

By ordering this shirt online I did miss out on the whole Ralph Lauren experience. When you visit a Ralph Lauren store, they transport you to an old-money world of leather sofas and tattered oriental rugs where all of the employees look like they're named Heathcliff and go to Oxford, even though they're probably named Kyle and go to a community college. So, when I ordered the shirt from my apartment while wearing boxers and eating cold pizza, a bit of the Ralph romance was lost.

Admittedly, this is a lot of shirt. You can't wear it very often, or else you'll quickly become known as "the shirt guy." It's the shirt you wear when you want a bit of attention or, conversely, when you feel totally void of any personality and are incapable of starting a conversation. The shirt will do the talking for you. However, if it does too much talking, you may end up getting punched.

I debuted the shirt at my local New York watering hole on a crowded evening. Within 0.05 seconds of entering the bar, I was in a headlock courtesy of the bar's owner, who was thrilled by the shirt, buying me a drink and demanding I have my photo taken with him. Throughout the evening there were several photos and many free drinks, and I even collected a few phone numbers. A blue button-down never got me this kind of action.

I'll definitely wear the shirt again, but when and where have yet to be determined. I must be careful, as it wields great power. I know too well that there's a fine line between patchwork and asshole.

This shirt will do the talking for you.

Rachel Antonoff *Clothing designer, Brooklyn*

REGRETTABLE ARTICLE OF CLOTHING: Cocktail dress

PURCHASED: Vermont, in 2010, for not much

TIMES WORN: 1

I'm not sure when people started calling secondhand stores "vintage shops." No matter what you call them, it's still someone's old clothes. In Vermont, where I bought this dress, they're usually secondhand or thrift stores. Vermont is big on maple syrup and skiing, not pretense.

In Vermont thrift stores, you're apt to find a lot more L.L.Bean than Geoffrey Beene, so I was surprised to find this 1980s ruffled cocktail dress wedged in among the racks. I suspected it probably once belonged to a weekend visitor versus someone who lived there year-round. You don't wear a lot of ruffles when kayaking or splitting logs.

The dress wasn't really my style, but I needed something to wear for New Year's Eve, an evening that gets way more attention than it deserves. And this was the dress it was getting.

I wore the dress to the aforementioned New Year's Eve party. I probably wasn't there more than ten minutes before I spilled an entire glass of wine down the front of it. I rang in the New Year damp but happy knowing I didn't spend a lot of money on a dress that was now ruined and that I'd no doubt never wear again.

Robby Doyle *Lifeguard/student, London and Chatham, Massachusetts*

REGRETTABLE ARTICLE OF CLOTHING: Fleece jacket

PURCHASED: Chatham, Massachusetts, in 2011, for $60

TIMES WORN: 20

It's not the fleece jacket itself that I regret—it's a perfectly fine jacket. But it's the secret shame this jacket carries that haunts me. This jacket, which I've worn on a fairly regular basis, originally belonged to my mom. There, I've said it. I feel so much better.

My mother bought the jacket when visiting me in the States and wore it often during her stay. When she was getting ready to leave, she didn't feel like lugging it back to London and asked me if I wanted it. "*Me*, wear a woman's jacket?" I tried it on, and it instantly became mine.

There weren't any features that would give away the fact that it was a lady's jacket—no rhinestone clasps or secret compartments to hold "personal-care items." The zipper is even on the right side, which I believe is traditionally the man's zipper side. In fact, the only people who could give away my secret were my siblings, who loved to taunt me with the fact that they knew "the dark truth of the fleece."

I realize I've jumped over the fact that my mother and I wear the same size clothes. The jacket was honestly a little big on her, and I'm not saying that just to assuage my ego. I'm currently not wearing any of my mother's other clothes, but I'm not ruling it out. I am English, after all.

My siblings loved to taunt me with the fact that they knew "the dark truth of the fleece."

The Brothers Mueller, Nate and Kirk *Art directors/*
digital designer dandies, Brooklyn

REGRETTABLE ARTICLE OF CLOTHING: Red and green brocade jackets

PURCHASED: Beijing, in 2006, for $50 each

TIMES WORN: 8

Yes, we are twins, and yes, we realize we are dressed alike. You'd be surprised how often we have to answer those questions.

We bought the jackets when visiting China. We went with different colors and slightly different patterns to mix things up. We've found the jackets are a little much to wear on their own. They work best when worn under a jacket like a vest, otherwise people start to assume we work at a very high-concept restaurant: "It's Chinese food with an all-twin staff!"

The fact that we dress alike probably comes from the fact that we have similar tastes, and in business, people remember us for it. It's become somewhat of our trademark. People wear uniforms in a lot of businesses; we just happen to choose our own every day. It's not as odd as it sounds, but if we start to spend our days sitting on a park bench yelling at pigeons, then we might worry. A little.

Gil Garcetti *Former district attorney/photographer, Los Angeles*

REGRETTABLE ARTICLE OF CLOTHING: Sweater-vest

PURCHASED: Los Angeles garage sale, in 1992, for 50¢

TIMES WORN: 3

I'm not a big garage-sale guy, but when I walk by one, I feel compelled to stop, not necessarily because of what's on sale but to watch the people. Garage-sale people are a certain breed. They seem to all know one another and speak their own garage-sale language. Some people get there at dawn, waiting for the garage door to open. Me, I prefer to sleep in—I don't really need a musical Christmas-tree stand or a used ThighMaster that badly.

The vest was in a box with a bunch of other old clothes. It had no size or indication of whether it was meant for a man or woman. For 50¢, I would take the chance. I'm pretty sure it was a guy's vest, although I could envision a female stand-up comic wearing it with a bolo tie in the '90s.

The few times I wore the vest, people asked me where I got it. They weren't looking to buy one for themselves; they were asking more out of curiosity as they sensed the vest had a backstory. I could have made up something more interesting, but I always told them the truth. In fact, when I told one of my best friends I got it at a garage sale, he said he assumed it must be something like that, because it looked like it belonged to a dead guy.

I'm pretty sure it was a guy's vest.

Elizabeth Cutler *Cofounder of SoulCycle, New York City*

REGRETTABLE ARTICLE OF CLOTHING: Seth Rogen T-shirt

PURCHASED: New York City, in 2014, for $20

TIMES WORN: 2

When you're a mom, you're a little more careful about what you wear than before you had kids. You want to set a good example, and you don't want to humiliate your kids by wearing something they'll be talking about in therapy twenty years from now. If I put something on that I'm not sure about, I ask myself if my own mother would wear it. The answer is inevitably "no," so then I ask my daughter. If I get an extended eye roll from her, it goes back in the closet.

The shirt in question was bought more as a joke. It features the many 420-loving faces of Seth Rogen. I wasn't sure if Seth signed off on this number or if it was more of a bootleg item, a fact that made it seem a little dangerous to wear.

I thought I could pull off wearing the shirt to a work function. You know, I'd seem like one of the cool kids. However, once I stepped out of the house, I was self-conscious as hell and kept pulling the blazer I was wearing closed.

One of my colleagues noticed the shirt and told me that she had recently seen someone wearing leggings featuring the face of James Franco, leading me to believe I may somehow have been duped into being part of a clever *Pineapple Express* viral marketing scheme.

Tim Convery *Owner of Tim-Scapes clothing company,*

Provincetown, Massachusetts

REGRETTABLE ARTICLE OF CLOTHING: Yeti suit

PURCHASED: Boston, in 2002, for $80

TIMES WORN: 20

Just to be clear, there is a definite difference between a yeti and Sasquatch. Sasquatch is brown, lives in forests, and apparently doesn't have very good hygiene—that is, if you trust the reports of loggers who've encountered him. Yetis, on the other hand, are white, live in the snow, and have adorable person-alities, if the one portrayed in the animated classic *Rudolph the Red-Nosed Reindeer* is any indication of their general demeanor. My suit was that of a yeti.

I bought the suit at a costume store on Charles Street to wear clubbing. I needed a new look. It wasn't exactly a high-quality garment; the massive "extremely flammable," label on its sleeve tipped me off to that. I believe it's a small mira-cle that I never became a human torch courtesy of a drunk girl's cigarette.

I got a fair amount of wear from the suit before it developed a horrible odor (see Sasquatch above), sort of a cross between a wet stuffed animal and a dirty swimming pool. Although, countless hours of wearing it while dancing to Depeche Mode could account for this. There was also a big furry head that was part of the suit, but someone stole it while I was attending a fairy convention in Tennessee. I bet I could probably find it if I went on eBay.

I needed a new look.

Chris Burch   *Entrepreneur/cofounder of Tory Burch, New York City*

REGRETTABLE ARTICLE OF CLOTHING: Sequined jacket

PURCHASED: Hong Kong, in 2005, for $500

TIMES WORN: 2

I had a bunch of these jackets made to give away to friends at a party, and I had a couple made for myself. The tailor did a great job, and everyone loved them. The only problem was that I didn't account for how heavy sequins could be. The jacket must have weighed twelve pounds. After walking around in it all night, I had a newfound respect for Siegfried and Roy. I just had to drink and make small talk while wearing it; those guys wear coats like this while dodging tigers.

I didn't account for how heavy sequins could be.

Bob Morris *Writer, Bellport, New York*

REGRETTABLE ARTICLE OF CLOTHING: Guatemalan tapestry pants

PURCHASED: Lake Atitlán, Guatemala, in 2003, for $75

TIMES WORN: 1

When you're traveling, it isn't your real life. The money is different, the food is different, and even how you shower is different. You're a little disoriented and prone to making some decisions you wouldn't normally make at home. That's how I'm rationalizing these pants.

Guatemalans are superb weavers. They make beautiful tapestries in the most amazing colors. On a trip to their country, I bought four panels, and while most people would bring them home to hang on the wall, I decided they should be pants. Yes, pants...that you wear on your legs. Also, I wanted the pants made before I left the country. I'm not sure why there was such a sense of urgency—maybe I knew if I got the panels home, I'd lose my enthusiasm for tapestry trousers and eventually they'd become table runners.

I found a very nice man who took on the absurd commission and completed the pants in a day. He did an amazing job. Even better, now I could tell people I had a tailor in Guatemala.

As soon as I got back to Manhattan, I wore the pants to a cocktail party. I discovered it was hard to walk around in them and even harder to weave my new Guatemalan tailor into the conversation. Nobody seemed to want to hear about my man Santiago in Lake Atitlán.

I've kept the pants, but I never wore them again. However, I'm convinced that someday Dries Van Noten or Thom Browne will feature Guatemalan panel pants on the runway. Then I can say I had mine first.

Claire Griffin *Sixth grader, Stonington, Connecticut*

REGRETTABLE ARTICLE OF CLOTHING: Ski pants

PURCHASED: Stowe, Vermont, in 2011, for $60

TIMES WORN: 8

I've never really been a pink person. I'm not sure why. Maybe it's because my grandmother used to try to give me Pepto-Bismol when I was sick. It was disgusting and the same color as these ski pants. Just kidding. I really don't think there's any big psychological reason why I don't like pink....and my ski pants.

I bought the pants on a family trip to Vermont. They didn't look that pink in the store. My sister warned me that they might look a lot pinker at home than in the store, but I didn't listen. As soon as I got them home, however, I knew there was a problem.

The pants were actually pretty comfortable and warm. It was just the color that was an issue. The first time I wore them, my uncle started making jokes: "Guess we won't lose Claire in any snow storms with those pants." "Here comes Claire, everybody put on your sunglasses." It was basically the same joke over and over. Why do people do that?

I got a little taller, so that was a good excuse to get a new pair of ski pants. I'll probably give the old pants away to somebody who likes pink.

By the way, my grandmother used to keep the Pepto-Bismol in the refrigerator. I just wanted to add that.

My sister warned me that they might look a lot pinker at home.

Gary Shteyngart *Writer/author of* Absurdistan *and* Super Sad
True Love Story, *New York City*

REGRETTABLE ARTICLE OF CLOTHING: Smoking jacket

PURCHASED: New York City, in the mid-1990s, for $79

TIMES WORN: 1

What else do you wear when you host a caviar party in a roach-infested apartment in Brooklyn in the '90s?

Linda Fargo *Fashion director at Bergdorf Goodman, New York City*

REGRETTABLE ARTICLE OF CLOTHING: Phillip Lim suit

PURCHASED: New York City, in 2012, for not sure

TIMES WORN: 1

My name is Linda, and I wore a hot pink suit. It's alright, I can talk about it now.

In most cities, wearing black is reserved for more somber or formal occasions, like weddings or funerals, but in New York it's practically a uniform. It never occurs to New Yorkers that to the rest of America, we look like an army of ninjas trudging down the street. So when I chose to wear a color—OK, a rather *bright* color—people noticed.

I wore the suit to a fashion event. I wasn't there very long. I stopped in, held a glass of white wine, had 4.3 conversations, and was back in the car in under an hour. Boom, done.

The next day, I started getting a lot of texts and e-mails I didn't understand: "Hey pink lady" and "I hear they can see you from outer space." I said there were a lot of messages—I didn't say they were all funny.

A little Googling revealed that some blogs had posted photos from the event I had attended the night before. The photos showed a sea of party guests in black and dark tones. However, one guest, wearing a suit the color of strawberry Twizzlers, stood out in every photo. Locating myself in the crowd was like the easiest game of *Where's Waldo?* in history.

The suit is actually quite lovely and fits me great. Maybe I'll wear it again someday if I have the right occasion. What that occasion might be, I have no idea.

Joey Jalleo *Vice President of Culture and Communications at Standard Hotels/Lord of The Boom Boom Room, Long Island City, New York*

REGRETTABLE ARTICLE OF CLOTHING: Red leather cowboy boots

PURCHASED: Santa Fe, New Mexico, in 2005, for $150

TIMES WORN: 4

When you visit Santa Fe, I believe you are legally obligated to buy one of three things: cowboy boots, a turquoise belt buckle, or a painting featuring a howling coyote that will one day be sold at a garage sale. I went with number one.

The cowboy boots were custom made, but not for me. I bought them at a resale shop. I knew nothing else about the boots, except that whomever owned them originally had different-sized feet. One boot was a size nine, the other a nine and a half.

This led me to believe that perhaps that's why they had the boots commissioned. The owner's life was likely plagued by bunions and blisters and ill-fitting flip-flops, and the boots were a way of finally celebrating their hideous deformity. While I salute embracing two different-sized feet, it forced me to find ways to try and make the larger boot fit. At various times, and with varying degrees of success, newspaper, tinfoil, and a wrapper from a Reese's Peanut Butter Cup were shoved into the toe of the larger boot. I finally went with wearing one very thick wool sock. It was hot but effective.

I decided to retire the boots, but not because of the size issue. I wore them out one night, and a *hilarious* friend asked me if I stole them off JonBenet Ramsey. I never looked at the boots the same way again. I should have gone with the belt buckle.

69

I knew nothing else about the boots, except that whomever owned them originally had different-sized feet.

Nick Potter *Attorney, New York City*

REGRETTABLE ARTICLE OF CLOTHING: Chinese jacket

PURCHASED: Beijing, in 2013, for $100

TIMES WORN: 8

China. It was all about China.

A few years ago, I went on a trip to China with my family. We had an amazing time, and after we got back, I became obsessed with all things Chinese: I got into Chinese cooking; I read up on Chinese art; I looked into taking Chinese-language courses. I did everything but buy a black-market panda and assemble an army of terra-cotta warriors in my basement to demonstrate my new love of all things Chinese.

Soon after the trip, I was invited to a wedding in Greenwich, Connecticut, a town that leans a wee bit on the formal side. I decided that instead of heeding the invitation's request of black-tie, I would forego a tuxedo and wear a silk Chinese jacket. I thought people would love it, and it would open up the door for me to share my endless fascinating stories and facts about China. "Why yes, you can buy a live crab from a vending machine in Guangzhou."

Sadly, the jacket wasn't the hit I expected. I got the obligatory pajama jokes, and a few people even asked if I wasn't aware the wedding was black-tie. (I believe that's called passive-aggressive.)

Over time, I've had to admit I may have gotten a bit carried away with my Chinese obsession. Now the jacket only comes out at home on special occasions. However, if you would like to discuss the difference between Cantonese and Mandarin, please let me know.

Sona Movsesian *Assistant to Conan O'Brien, Los Angeles*

REGRETTABLE ARTICLE OF CLOTHING: Sue Wong dress

PURCHASED: Bloomingdale's at the Beverly Center, Los Angeles, in 2003, for $250

TIMES WORN: 2

For me, 2003 was the year of the wedding. Not my own, but the others I had to attend. It was right after college, and my wardrobe consisted primarily of sweatshirts and jeans, so I needed to buy a dress.

One wedding was in Los Angeles and the other in Australia, so I thought I'd go with something a little more beachy and bohemian. That could explain why I chose a dress that Stevie Nicks might wear if she took up figure skating. The dress was not remotely flattering to my body, and the beads stitched all over it kept getting caught in my hair, even causing me to cry out in pain during one of the ceremonies. It wasn't a loud scream—more of a surprised yelp, like when you step on a dog's tail.

People complimented me on the dress, but I have a feeling they felt they just had to say *something*. This is not a dress that can easily be ignored. It combines colors, textures, and fabrics while also playing with proportions and hemlines. I believe the technical term for the dress is "a friggin' mess."

Because of the dress, I now feel sympathy for celebrities who get skewered for what they wear on the red carpet. They can at least blame their stylists; I had no one to blame but myself. OK, I blame my mother a little, as she was there when I bought the thing and could have stopped me.

After wearing it to the two weddings, I retired the dress, but its specter lingers. I occasionally see myself wearing it in wedding photos displayed in friends' homes. Without fail, they always point and say, "There you are, in *that* dress."

73

I chose a dress that Stevie Nicks might wear if she took up figure skating.

Bill Thomas *Founder of Bill's Khakis, Reading, Pennsylvania*

REGRETTABLE ARTICLE OF CLOTHING: Letter sweater

PURCHASED: Pottstown, Pennsylvania, in 1975, for $40

TIMES WORN: 30

Human. Horrific. Hunchback. Husky. Herbivore. When you wear a sweater with a massive H on the chest, you know you're begging for comments. Over the years, I've heard some pretty funny ones and others I probably shouldn't repeat. "What superpowers do you have?" "Are you on *Sesame Street*?" A lot of people assume my name must begin with *H* and insist on guessing it even after I tell them it does not. If they're really persistent, I just play along: "Yup, you guessed it, my name *is* Horatio."

The *H* actually stands for *Hill*, the name of the boarding school I went to in Pennsylvania. It was the sweater I bummed around in on campus and wore to sporting events. All my friends had them, too. It was sort of a precursor to today's hoodie.

74

I realize the sweater has a bit of a *Brideshead* factor, but if I don't carry around a stuffed bear, I can usually pull it off. More than anything, I'm just proud that the sweater still fits me. So in that case, the *H* stands for *Hell, yeah!*

Tania Debono   *Multimedia artist, New York City and Sydney*

REGRETTABLE ARTICLE OF CLOTHING: Lavender jacket/dress

PURCHASED: Berlin, in 2014, for $300

TIMES WORN: 2

This was my attempt to integrate pastels into my wardrobe. I generally like things a bit more somber and severe, so I made a conscious decision to bring the colors of after-dinner mints into my world. I soon learned that that was a bad idea. Pastels seem to only work on females under the age of six or over the age of sixty.

Also, when I bought it in Berlin, there was some question as to what exactly this garment was. Is it a jacket? A dress? Is it some odd German hybrid? I'm still not quite sure. It's too heavy to be a dress, and as a coat there are probably four days a year temperature-wise when it would be appropriate.

Besides all that, it doesn't fit me. It is four sizes too big and swallows me up. I thought with the right shoes I could pull it off. I've yet to find those magical shoes.

Whenever I've taken it out of the closet and considered wearing it, my boyfriend lets out a sigh, which I've come to know as "the sigh of hate." It's the same sigh he reserves for whenever I ask him to unload the dishwasher or see a Kristen Stewart movie.

Chris Benz *Creative director of Bill Blass, Brooklyn*

REGRETTABLE ARTICLE OF CLOTHING: Comme des Garçons rabbit-ear baseball cap

PURCHASED: Comme des Garçons boutique, Tokyo, in 2013, for $525

TIMES WORN: 1

I had been spending a lot of time in Tokyo, a city that is no stranger to fashion risks. You see girls (and boys) dressed as Little Bo Beep, French maids carrying parasols and yes, that was a guy using a hollowed-out baby doll as a backpack. So maybe I had become immune to realizing a leather baseball cap with bunny ears wasn't a terribly wise purchase.

The hat was featured in the Comme des Garçons fall runway show and had gotten a lot of buzz. OK, buzz in fashion circles, not in real-people circles. It's not as if they were discussing it on the streets of Omaha. But for a fashion person like myself, it was something I coveted. Fashion people covet things, it's what we do. Or maybe we just like to use the word *covet*.

When I bought the hat, I gave little thought as to where I'd be wearing it. Sure, if I was invited to an Easter egg hunt at a leather bar, I'd have just the thing, but for my day-to-day life, it probably didn't make sense. Would it even fit on the subway? Also, I knew the guys who hung out at my local bodega might take issue with it. Life would not be worth living if every time I went on a Funyuns and SmartWater run, I was taunted by the call of "Yo, Bugs Bunny!"

If I was invited to an Easter egg hunt at a leather bar, I'd have just the thing.

Cressida Leyshon *Deputy fiction editor at* The New Yorker,

New York City

REGRETTABLE ARTICLE OF CLOTHING: Pink overcoat

PURCHASED: New York City, in 2006, for $100

TIMES WORN: 1

In almost every horror movie, there is a moment when a person debates whether to open a door, fearing what waits on the other side. In my personal horror movie, a pink overcoat with embroidered trim awaits me.

I bought the coat on my lunch hour at a sample sale set up in some random garment-district office building. I'm never sure who runs those sales or where they get the merchandise, and it's probably wise not to ask. I have a feeling those operations are somehow related to the guys who sell purses off blankets on Canal Street.

I wasn't really sure of the coat, but I bought it anyway and carried it back to my office in a crumpled brown paper bag as if it were something illicit. I hung the coat in the closet in my office and left it there. Every time I opened the closet door, there it was, still wearing its tags, mocking me. Each time I saw it, I would ask myself why I bought it and tell myself I should either wear it or get rid of it. Neither seemed to happen.

Every couple of years I would move offices and each time the coat came with me. I hid it behind another coat that I actually wore, but all I needed to see was a sliver of pink to remind me of my unnecessary, unfortunate purchase.

Recently, I moved to a new office building many blocks from my old office. It was the perfect opportunity to purge everything I didn't want or need, which I did. Except for the coat. The coat still hangs in my office closet today. If you'd like it, stop by and it's yours.

James Whiteside *Principal dancer at American Ballet Theatre, New York City*

REGRETTABLE ARTICLE OF CLOTHING: Overalls

PURCHASED: East Village, New York, in 2012, for $15

TIMES WORN: 2

I own two types of clothes: fancy adult clothes to wear to fancy adult functions and T-shirts and jeans. I don't seem to have any in-between, normal-person clothes. I don't think I could ever be one of those guys in khakis and a button-down. I'd end up accessorizing the look with feather angel wings or Bedazzle the pants. I'm pretty sure that's not what the Brooks Brothers had in mind.

I like things other people might consider weird—thus, these salute-to-Easter overalls. I bought them at a thrift store in the East Village where I've found a lot of great things: an Amish straw hat, a purse that's also a horse, and a giant kitty-cat rhinestone brooch.

The one big regret I have about the overalls is that they don't really fit me. The bib comes halfway up my chest, and the straps don't come anywhere near my shoulders. I have some rainbow *Godspell* suspenders I could fashion into straps, but I think that might betray the overall mood of the overalls.

I noticed the other day that I forgot to remove the price tag from the overalls. I think I'll leave it on and see if it becomes a trend. If it does, I'll be tweeting the hell out of the fact that I was doing it first.

Julie Rice *Cofounder of SoulCycle, New York City*

REGRETTABLE ARTICLE OF CLOTHING: Cork Christian Louboutin shoes

PURCHASED: Jeffrey in New York City, in 2012, for $350

TIMES WORN: 1

Jeffrey is an amazing store that brings all the best clothes in the world together under one roof. It's like Whole Foods, but with Gucci and Balenciaga instead of quinoa. They have an annual sale, and attending it is something I feel I need to do for my personal well-being—it's get my teeth cleaned, visit a place I've never been before, go to the Jeffrey sale. I do these things once a year.

Seven-inch-high cork-soled wedges weren't something I necessarily needed in my wardrobe, but for the price, I thought they were a smart choice. Although once I got them home and tried to walk in them, I learned they were a dangerous choice. Seven inches is really high. You start to sway a little like a skyscraper in heavy winds. I envisioned myself trying to walk across the cobblestone streets of Lower Manhattan and instantly saw skinned knees, a spilled purse, and giggling tourists posting videos online. Cut to shoes going back in the box.

The shoes have become my daughter's favorite thing to wear when playing dress-up. She and her friends love to put them on and teeter around the house. Whenever they do, in the back of my mind I always wonder, Does our insurance policy cover this?

Seven inches is really high. You start to sway like a skyscraper in heavy winds.

Adam Green _Musician/artist/filmmaker, Brooklyn, NY_

REGRETTABLE ARTICLE OF CLOTHING: Traditional Swiss Alpine farmer shirt

PURCHASED: Zurich, Switzerland, in 2013, for $160

TIMES WORN: 4

American farmers like to wear overalls and John Deere caps. Swiss farmers, on the other hand, like to wear charming red embroidered shirts and peaked, brimmed wool hats. I learned this when my band was on tour in Switzerland.

Also, while in Switzerland, I discovered a liqueur called Appenzeller. If you ever see it at a bar, order it. Actually, order a lot of it. It's the Swiss version of Jägermeister and pretty amazing. One afternoon, after a fair amount of Appenzeller, my friend Oskar decided that what I needed to go with my buzz was a true Alpine outfit. Soon we were zigzagging, reversing, backtracking, and spinning out through the back roads of Zurich in search of a clothing store open on the weekend.

We found an open shop that was exactly what we were looking for. It was absurdly quaint. If somebody told us that all the people in the store went back to living in a cuckoo clock at night, we would have totally believed them. I bought my "edelweiss shirt" and wore it at my concert that night, much to the delight of the local crowd.

I swore I would wear the shirt when I got back home. That didn't happen. It went straight into my closet, where it sat for a long time. One day when my wife was doing some spring-cleaning, she decided it was time for the shirt to go. I begged her to let me keep it. She agreed on the condition that I wear the shirt at least once a year. So now every year I have a weird day where I dress like a Swiss farmer. Maybe this year I'll even try to rent a cow.

My friend Oskar decided that what I needed to go with my buzz was a true Alpine outfit.

Flannery Rogers *Oyster farmer, Falmouth, Massachusetts*

REGRETTABLE ARTICLE OF CLOTHING: Dress

PURCHASED: Boston, in 2012, for $100

TIMES WORN: 1

This dress begs a lot of questions.

First, is it really a dress? The top and bottom look completely unrelated, but it is, in fact, one piece.

Second, is the bottom of the dress a map of somewhere? I've Googled and searched, and I've yet to find any location that matches up, so I doubt there is some *National Treasure* mystery map hidden within the fabric. It would be cool if there were, though.

Finally, why did I buy the dress? I never wear dresses, but something compelled me to buy this one at a vintage store on Newbury Street. I may have to go with laziness and the fact that I hate to shop but I needed something for New Year's Eve. I believe my resolution that year was to never wear the dress again.

Dennis Gronim *Blues guitarist, Brooklyn*

REGRETTABLE ARTICLE OF CLOTHING: Djellaba

PURCHASED: Milan, in 1994, for $300

TIMES WORN: 4

I've always wanted a djellaba, not just because it's fun to say but also because they looked rather comfortable and you can carry bread, a chicken, or contraband in their roomy hood.

I'd been traveling in Morocco, where djellabas are everyday street wear, and I visited Milan soon after. I decided that if I was going to get a djellaba, I should do it right and have one made. Milan seemed like a good place to do that.

I wandered the streets of Milan and chatted with some tailors. A few couldn't understand English, and others couldn't understand why I'd want a djellaba. I finally found one who understood what I wanted and gave me a price of $75 to make the djellaba of my dreams.

90

Next, I set out on a quest for fabric. I decided to splurge a little on some really beautiful merino wool, as I knew this would be my one and only djellaba. Soon I would have the Cadillac of djellabas, the djellaba that all other djellabas would be judged against.

I returned to the tailor and had all my measurements taken. The tailor even commented on my exquisite choice of fabric.

I returned a couple of days later to pick up my finished garment. I tried it on, and it was magnificent. The tailor then presented me with a bill for $300. "Wait, what happened to $75?" I asked. The tailor said he had no recollection of quoting me that price, and I soon realized that my choice of fancy fabric had made him think he could charge me a lot. Damn. I was victim of a con-job-djellaba.

I decided that if I was going to get a djellaba, I should do it right and have one made.

Katie Stoller *Producer, Austin, Texas*

REGRETTABLE ARTICLE OF CLOTHING: Vintage metallic gown

PURCHASED: Williamsburg, Brooklyn, in 2007, for $35

TIMES WORN: 1

At the time I bought this dress, I was obsessed with the movie *Bob & Carol & Ted & Alice*. If you haven't seen it, I highly recommend it—if you're into Natalie Wood, poolside martinis, and fabulous '70s fashion. And who isn't?

I imagined myself wearing the dress to some groovy beach party in Malibu, but I ended up wearing it to a New Year's Eve party in a five-story walk-up in Williamsburg. The party was at some beardo's apartment, which had a flashing Dos Equis sign in the living room and a huge fish tank with no fish. Natalie, save me.

After the party, we ended up at a McDonald's in the West Village that is notorious for crazy people. Sure enough, I was somehow dragged into breaking up a fight between two spray-tanned muscle heads and got a Diet Coke spilled all over the dress. However, I was proud I managed to finish all my fries. It's the little victories in life that matter.

I think the dress deserves a second chance. So when I'm in my sixties and move to a condo in Boca with my girlfriends, I've decided the dress will be my go-to outfit whenever I have the gang over for whiskey sours and Yahtzee.

93

Michael Phillips Moskowitz _Entrepreneurship fellow at Harvard Kennedy School, New York City_

REGRETTABLE ARTICLE OF CLOTHING: Marching-band jacket

PURCHASED: Los Angeles, in 2012, for $45

TIMES WORN: 2

I'm assuming the jacket once belonged to a member of a marching band or a majorette. I bought it at a vintage store in Silver Lake, so I'm not exactly sure of its provenance. (That's the fancy word for who owned it before me, right?) The jacket strangely fits me incredibly well, so maybe it belonged to me in a former life. Though that's probably not true, as I'm a disaster at baton twirling.

The jacket is emblazoned with a Spartan, so a Michigan State student might have owned it, as I believe that's their mascot. I see a fresh-faced kid from the Midwest coming out to make it big in Hollywood, then forced to sell his or her jacket to survive, big dreams just a memory. Or there just wasn't room in their closet.

I wore it out once with a T-shirt underneath. I treated it like it was a jean jacket. I expected a lot of comments, but didn't get any. That's how I knew it was bad. Friends who are normally happy to throw barbs my way when I sport something a little fashion-forward said nothing. I never know how to get a reaction out of people anymore.

95

Cipriana Quann *Cofounder and editor in chief of* Urban Bush

Babes/*contributing writer for* Vogue.com, *Brooklyn*

REGRETTABLE ARTICLE OF CLOTHING: Gold jumpsuit

PURCHASED: Vintage store, New York, in 2011, for $20

TIMES WORN: 1

Every time I look at this jumpsuit, "U Can't Touch This" starts playing in my head. And now that I've mentioned it, you no doubt have one of MC Hammer's greatest hits playing in your head as well. Sorry about that.

When I bought the jumpsuit, I wasn't aware of its parachute-pants nature. Maybe its glimmering fabric dazzled me, but it seemed catsuit-ish and stream-lined when I tried it on. It's not. When you're standing still it's fine, but any movement and it begins to billow and fill up with air. This is not a flattering look.

I occasionally take the jumpsuit out of the closet (cue music) and hope that somehow it has magically transformed itself and is now cured of the billowing problem. I could take it to a tailor to be fixed, but tailors always charge a million dollars even if they just move a button. I realize it's a skill, but come on, there really needs to be a chain of discount tailors somewhere. (Note to self: Start discount-tailor chain.)

I've only worn the jumpsuit once and got mixed reactions, so unless I decide to have it radically altered, that may be its only outing. I think that's all the Hammer time a girl may need.

It seemed catsuit-ish and streamlined when I tried it on.

Yvonne Force Villareal *Cofounder of Art Production Fund/ founding partner of Culture Corps, New York City and Marfa, Texas*

REGRETTABLE ARTICLE OF CLOTHING: Mr. Blackwell custom coat

PURCHASED: San Francisco, in 2013, for $300

TIMES WORN: 1

"The return of Mrs. Roper" is what my husband calls this coat. If you aren't familiar with **Mrs. Roper**, she was the fabulous downstairs neighbor on *Three's Company* who had a volcanic sense of fashion. I Googled her recently and think all of her outfits would still look great today—all they'd need is the right styling.

This coat is vintage Mr. Blackwell, an acclaimed 1960s designer famous for elegant pieces and his yearly Worst-Dressed List, which was the first brilliantly bitchy takedown of celebs with really bad style. He described Martha Stewart as looking like "the centerfold of the *Farmers' Almanac*." Back then people were polite, so he was quite shocking.

I've put on the coat a number of times, but it never makes it out my front door. I thought with the whole new-haute-hippie-chic thing I could pull it off, but then my husband rolls his eyes again, and it's back to the closet for the coat. For a small movement, the eye-roll truly yields great power.

Brian Latimer *Arborist, West Falmouth, Massachusetts*

REGRETTABLE ARTICLE OF CLOTHING: Tommy Hilfiger jacket

PURCHASED: New York City, in 2010, for $8

TIMES WORN: 2

Considering I only paid $8 for the jacket, I can't be that upset it didn't work out. I mean, $8 is half an hour of parking in Boston or half a martini in New York. I got a whole jacket.

I bought the jacket at one of those stores on Canal Street in New York City where you assume everything in the store fell off a truck. The guy running the store kept trying to sell me a *Dora the Explorer* wristwatch and boxer shorts emblazoned with a giant winking smiley face. It worried me that I looked like someone who might be in the market for either.

I thought the jacket would be good for snowboarding, but there was one problem. The jacket was made out of some futuristic—cheap—fabric that was like a cross between a trash bag and one of those silver blankets marathon runners wrap around themselves so that everybody knows they've just run a marathon. Whatever the chemistry involved, it resulted in a fabric so slippery that if I fell on the mountain, there was no way to stop. I was transformed into a human luge, bulleting down the slopes at tremendous speeds, taking out everything in my path. There's a Dutch family out there somewhere who can attest to this.

I've never been too sure that the jacket was actually a genuine Tommy Hilfiger, either. I have a feeling that if I looked closely at the label, the word *Tommy* might be spelled with three *M*s.

103

The fabric was a cross between a trash bag and one of those silver blankets marathon runners wrap around themselves.

Anne Levine *Radio talk-show host, Dennis, Massachusetts*

REGRETTABLE ARTICLE OF CLOTHING: Embroidered shirt

PURCHASED: Miami, Florida, in 1985, for $100

TIMES WORN: 1

I bought this shirt to wear to Easter dinner at the home of my then-boyfriend Igor's parents. Igor was Ukrainian, and I thought the shirt had just the right amount of Easter bling mixed with a dash of Eastern European playfulness. I also thought it would allow for ease of movement if I were forced to participate in an egg hunt.

In addition to Igor's parents, the dinner guests included a crew of people named Irka, Balaban, Olga, and Mikal. When we sat down, I knew my small-talk abilities would be tested in a major way. The table was set with baroque silver, gaudy china, gilt-edged crystal, and heavy brocade napkins. The vibe was half Nicholas and Alexandra, half Tony and Carmela.

As we ate dinner, I soon realized there would be no egg hunts or marshmallow Peeps at this Easter celebration. Shots of vodka replaced jellybeans for this crowd. I did my best to understand everyone's heavy Ukrainian accents, but once the vodka began to flow, I pretty much gave up. When a new topic of conversation was introduced, I would follow the lead of the room and smile, nod, giggle, or frown along with everyone else. I will always wonder what topics I was agreeing with that day—"black market ivory trading, sure, why not?"

When I was leaving, carrying Tupperware containers full of food I'd never eat, one of the women commented on my shirt: "You look like pretty little girl," she said, but with her heavy accent, it sounded suspiciously like "pretty little gorilla." That's one more thing I'll always wonder about.

Mikey DeTemple *Pro surfer/filmmaker, Brooklyn*

REGRETTABLE ARTICLE OF CLOTHING: Pendleton popover shirt

PURCHASED: Montauk, New York, in 2014, for $5

TIMES WORN: 1

There's something vaguely Peter Pan about this shirt. I think it's the weirdly long pointed collar combined with the short zippered front.

I bought the shirt at Bob Melet's Epic Yard Sale, which is like the Oscars for people who care about clothes. Bob runs Melet Mercantile, an appointment-only shop in Manhattan that carries the coolest vintage stuff in the world. Once a year, he has a huge sale out at the beach that has people lining up before dawn waiting to get their hands on old doctor's bags, reindeer-skin parkas, and ancient Navajo-blanket ponchos. You see celebrities and regular people searching through the piles and racks. "Look, there's Jerry Seinfeld trying on a coonskin cap!"

There were tons of other things at the sale that I wanted to buy, but the boy-who-refused-to-grow-up shirt was more in my price range. There was a lot I liked about the shirt, but the damn collar ruined everything. Thus, my chances of ever wearing it again are next to Neverland.

The damn collar ruined everything.

Michael Moore *Special events director, New York City*

REGRETTABLE ARTICLE OF CLOTHING: Flowered shirt

PURCHASED: China, in 2013, for $80

TIMES WORN: 5

Some people get asked, "Does the carpet match the drapes?" In my case, the question is, "Why does your shirt match the tablecloth?"

I was visiting China and went on something of a buying frenzy. There was so much great stuff, and I was going to see just how much I could fit in my luggage. China is a very large country, and I intended to bring home a big chunk of it.

I found this beautiful antique fabric at a market. I was told the fabric was originally used to make kimonos. I wasn't sure if I was in need of a kimono, but I knew I wanted the fabric. I bought it in a few colors and figured I would decide later what it would become.

When I got back to New York City, I had a tablecloth made from the fabric. I had bought a fair amount of it, so I decided to have a shirt made as well. Actually, with the amount of fabric I bought I could also have probably made a shower curtain, a swimming-pool cover, and a couple of yoga mats, too.

The tailor did a great job on the shirt. However, people always assumed it was a Hawaiian shirt, and I'd have to set them straight. Then the next thing you know, I'd be in an hour-long discussion of the Qing Dynasty. One person even asked if I bought the shirt at Tommy Bahama—I'm still recovering from that.

Paige Novick *Jewelry designer, New York City*

REGRETTABLE ARTICLE OF CLOTHING: Child's sweater

PURCHASED: Ralph Lauren store in East Hampton, New York, in 2002 for $175

TIMES WORN: About 6

It wasn't my fault—I'm blaming Carrie Bradshaw. In the early 2000s, when everybody's favorite size 000 started baring her midriff on *Sex and the City*, finding the smallest clothes possible and proving you could squeeze into them became the thing to do. It was almost like a challenge. Baby tees and shrunken shirts were everywhere. I fully believe there's somebody somewhere who wore her dog's sweater. It was that ridiculous.

I opted for a children's size 5 flag-motif crewneck sweater. It would have been adorable on a first grader, but not so much on someone drinking a martini at the bar at the Four Seasons. It also didn't help that I paired it with the lowest of low-rise jeans. I walked down the street like this. I had family and friends and coworkers who cared about me, and yet none of them stopped me. Where were you people?

I'm not sure why I've held onto the sweater. Maybe I subconsciously keep it to remind myself to resist trendy fashion faux pas in the future. At least I didn't wear a pink tutu and stand on the corner waiting to be splashed by a passing bus. That often.

111

It would have been adorable on a first grader.

Peter Davis *Editor/writer, New York City*

REGRETTABLE ARTICLE OF CLOTHING: Hate sweater

PURCHASED: Supreme store in New York City, in 2013, for about $200

TIMES WORN: 1

When I first saw the sweater, I thought it had the word *hair* written all over it. Then I realized it said *hate*. Others might say they bought the sweater as some big social statement, but me, I bought it because it fit well and was the colors of Good & Plenty.

The sweater is from Supreme. Supreme is a very cool brand that has a huge cult following among skateboarders, and they only make a few of every item. So on the day things are released, you need to get there early in order to snag them from under the scores of 19-year-old longboarders. People stand in line to get in the store. It's sort of like trying to get into a club, except fewer people are yelling, "Pick me! Pick me!"

Once I owned the sweater, deciding where to wear it was the hard part. I knew I needed a hate-friendly crowd. Thus, I wore it for an event during New York Fashion Week. People reacted to the sweater a little too well, and I found myself having to have the same conversation over and over. A few people wanted to engage in heady discussions as to the meaning of the sweater, something I wasn't really interested in doing. You never have that problem when you wear a white V-neck T-shirt.

I wore it during Fashion Week.

Chris and Meggie Kempner *Owners of KEMPNER NYC,*

New York City

REGRETTABLE ARTICLE OF CLOTHING: Toile pants (him), sequin dress (her)

PURCHASED: Nantucket, Massachusetts, in 2005, for $175 (him); New York City, in 2013, for $200 (her)

TIMES WORN: 4 (him), 1 (her)

CHRIS: I think the most amazing thing about these pants is that I didn't get punched in the face when I wore them. I mean, if I saw me wearing these pants, I'd want to punch me in the face.

I bought the pants on Nantucket, a rarefied little island where dressing like a tool is embraced and celebrated. You see pants embroidered with whales, martinis, and sailboats on every corner. If for some reason Nantucket should ever gain independence, lime green and hot pink would be the colors of its flag.

The pants in question are made from upholstery fabric. It was a thing, briefly in the early 2000s, to own a pair of these, and yes, I succumbed to preppy peer pressure. However, I did have the good sense to never wear them off the island, otherwise this story may have ended differently (see above: face punching).

MEGGIE: I was invited to a bachelorette party in Las Vegas. I had never been there, but I knew enough about it from Scorsese movies and reality TV to know that it's a place where taste takes a holiday. I needed a dress that would allow me to fit in.

Finding a Las Vegas–friendly dress in New York City was harder than I thought. Things were either too prom-ish or immediately brought to mind *Pretty Woman*. I reluctantly settled on the green sequins and got on the plane. One thing I didn't factor in was the heat—it was absurdly hot that weekend, and with the dress on, I felt like I was wearing one of those sauna suits that wrestlers wear to lose weight. I spent a lot of time searching for air-conditioning.

I was mistaken for a cocktail waitress twice while I was there, so I guess the dress was a success in terms of my passing as a local. If I wore it out in New York City, I'm not sure what I'd be mistaken for, but I have a couple of pretty good guesses.

115

Maxwell Britten *Bar director at Maison Premiere, Brooklyn*

REGRETTABLE ARTICLE OF CLOTHING: Vintage team jacket

PURCHASED: New York City, in 2004, for $30

TIMES WORN: 5

I decided this jacket was reversible. It wasn't. The original jacket I bought was more of a basic green shiny baseball jacket. Then I made my little discovery of the jacket's lining. There was this secret Hawaiian paradise hiding inside, so I wore the jacket inside out.

Aside from two hyper-observant friends, nobody ever noticed I had reversed the jacket. And when they asked why the zipper pull was on the inside, I gave them some long, complicated answer that would deter them from asking any more questions.

These days, I dress more like one of Don Draper's inner circle, but there was a time when I was more free-form with my wardrobe. Some might say I had yet to find my own personal style, while others would call it wearing some really crazy shit. This jacket is from that period in my life.

I have a feeling if I showed up at a bar to meet Don Draper wearing this jacket, he'd take a sip from his Manhattan, stare straight ahead, and say, "Rethink the coat, kid."

Mike Nouveau *DJ, Manhattan*

REGRETTABLE ARTICLE OF CLOTHING: Black skirt

PURCHASED: Comme des Garçons, in 2008, for $450

TIMES WORN: 10

I wasn't trying to make any big statement by wearing a skirt. Believe me, it was not part of some gender-bending revolt against pants. I like wearing skirts when I'm in the mood; they're comfortable, and they look pretty cool. Also, a guy wearing a skirt pisses off the right people, which I somewhat enjoy.

I'd owned some skirts before, but this one was particularly short. I decided it was probably wise to wear leggings underneath it, or else one gust of wind could get me brought up on morality charges.

In 2008 wearing a skirt was a little unexpected, but today you see a lot of skirts in men's runway shows, and a lot of hip-hop guys are wearing them. Oh, and Jaden Smith wore a skirt to his prom—the fact that I know that troubles me.

I decided it was wise to wear leggings underneath it.

Annamarie Tendler Mulaney *Makeup artist/author of*

The Daily Face, *Los Angeles*

REGRETTABLE ARTICLE OF CLOTHING: Blue velvet dress

PURCHASED: Wasteland in Studio City, in 2012, for $70

TIMES WORN: 5

When I bought this dress, the girl at the cash register said, "This dress has been here a long time, and no one has been brave enough to buy it. I'm glad it has a home now." At that moment, I felt a sense of pride knowing that I'm the type of person who is willing to take in the fashion misfits, someone who welcomes clothes that others shun or cast off. Bring me your brocade jumpsuits, your leopard pillbox hats, your tangerine lace maxi dresses—they all have a place in my closet.

I understand that not everyone would have a need in her life for a vintage blue velvet gown embellished with sequined metallic cranes. (Yes, those are cranes!) It's not something you'd throw on to run out to Pink Dot. But why dress like everyone else? Show a little fashion bravery.

The only problem with this dress is that it can get rather warm. Los Angeles, I've learned, is not a velvet-friendly town.

Yes, those are cranes.

Sid Karger *Screenwriter/Director, New York City*

REGRETTABLE ARTICLE OF CLOTHING: Cashmere sweater

PURCHASED: St. Barts, in 2010, for $600

TIMES WORN: 4

In the same way they warn you about eating before swimming, I feel there should be a warning about drinking before shopping.

I bought this sweater while on vacation in St. Barts. For those not familiar with St. Barts, it's a beautiful and ridiculous resort island where a bowl of soup costs $30 and you encounter the most random celebrity sightings at every turn. Oh look, Judge Judy is splitting a Cobb salad with Jay Z!

On a cloudy day, in lieu of going to the beach, we went to lunch. At lunch, we drank wine—lots of wine, wine of various colors and from many countries. It was after this that shopping seemed like a good idea.

I have no idea why, but I immediately wanted the sweater when I saw it in the shop. I can't even blame a pushy salesperson. It was me who decided I needed a lavender cashmere sweater slapped with the face of everybody's favorite Marxist revolutionary, Che Guevara.

I wore the sweater a few times, but I was always nervous. I knew it would be, as my Aunt Betty might say, "a real conversation starter." I decided to retire the sweater after a woman at a party told me she loved my Mandy Patinkin sweater. I'm guessing she meant from his *Chicago Hope* years.

There should be a warning about drinking before shopping.

Nick Wooster *Street-style icon/fashion consultant, New York City*

REGRETTABLE ARTICLE OF CLOTHING: Craig Green shirt and pants

PURCHASED: Barneys, New York, in 2010, for $800

TIMES WORN: A ton

This outfit was a mystery to be solved. I was a sartorial Sherlock, and I would not rest until I had the solution. However, I chose to forego the deerstalker cap and meerschaum pipe in the process—though it is a strong look.

I bought these two pieces not really knowing how I was going to wear them or if I ever would. They were unlike anything I owned. Sometimes I see something that I have to have regardless of what it looks like on me. My need to do this no doubt fits nicely into some textbook pathology, but that's another mystery for another day.

The pants and shirt worn together immediately took you into the clerical world, and regret started knocking at my door. They were such cool pieces, but I couldn't figure out how to pull them off. Then I had a eureka moment—I just needed to break them up! Worn separately, they looked amazing. These pants I once regretted are now one of my favorite pairs. OK, I realize that's not as dramatic as the solution to *The Hound of the Baskervilles*, but for me it seemed pretty major on a Tuesday afternoon.

Annabella Hochschild *Writer, New York City*

REGRETTABLE ARTICLE OF CLOTHING: Crayon dress

PURCHASED: St. Mark's Place, New York City, in 2014, for $8

TIMES WORN: 2

There is a definite distinction between a crayon costume and a crayon dress. The costume generally comes in a bag, is made of gossamer-thin acetate, and has a hat that looks like a small traffic cone. The dress, on the other hand, is sold on a hanger, is made of formfitting carcinogenic foam, and can cost as much as $10. I own the latter.

I bought the dress at one of the last remaining stores in New York City that feels a little dangerous. Maybe they have dogfights in the basement on weekends or deal homemade LSD called Mind Detergent. You just know something else is going on there.

Before I actually bought the dress, I visited it a couple of times. I was a little apprehensive about buying it because of *them*. The group of scary but cool punk kids who hang out at the corner of my street in the East Village and silently judge everyone. These aren't poseurs from the suburbs who cut the sleeves off their Hollister shirts and ride *Angry Birds* skateboards. These dudes are the real deal.

The first time I wore the dress, I had a rather late night/morning, and the birds were chirping and the garbage trucks groaning as I neared my apartment. As I reached my corner, I saw them. I tried being as nonchalant as possible as I walked by, but I linked eyes with one of the group's leaders. He wore a Meat Puppets T-shirt and an air of superiority. I gave him a little head nod that said, "I respect who you are, and please don't hurt me." He then looked me up and down, raised his Dunkin Donuts Styrofoam cup, smiled, and said, "Sick."

At that moment, I knew—they liked me, they really liked me.

Spencer Means *Real estate broker, Upper West Side, New York City*

REGRETTABLE ARTICLE OF CLOTHING: Sable muffler

PURCHASED: Henry Cowit in New York City, in 2013, for $1,200

TIMES WORN: 4

When you're shopping and come upon something that isn't the most practical purchase, it's wise to bring a friend along to help you rationalize why you need to own it. Case in point: this sable muffler.

I was shopping with a friend when I saw the muffler. I started with how cold it gets in New York City and how warm the muffler would be. She agreed. Next, I moved on to how the color was perfect and would match so many things in my wardrobe. I got a "yes" on that as well. Finally, I hit her with the fact that I hadn't bought myself anything extravagant in a long time. I was pulling out my credit card before she finished nodding.

I've found I have to know my audience when I wear the muffler. If I sense I may be among antifur people, I might say it's "faux fur" if asked. Getting paint thrown on you can really ruin your day.

There's also a lot of talk as to what exactly a sable is. Is it in the mink family? Is it a rodent? Is it from Russia? Probably the best response came from my shopping-partner friend. When asked, "What is a sable?" she replied, "Damn expensive."

131

What exactly is a sable?

Virginia Elwood *Tattoo artist, Brooklyn*

REGRETTABLE ARTICLE OF CLOTHING: Fringed buckskin pants

PURCHASED: Ralph Lauren, in 2014, for price purposely forgotten

TIMES WORN: 1

I don't think there's anything wrong with buying clothes for fantasy you. Fantasy you is the person or persons you imagine yourself being. And of course these fantasy people would need a different wardrobe than you. For instance, if I imagined myself as Secretary of State, I'd no doubt have a lot of power suits and sensible heels. Or if I were a soccer mom, my closet would be full of fleece vests and elastic-waist jeans. These buckskin pants are for rock-and-roll me.

I bought the pants at Ralph Lauren. Ralph Lauren is a very good place to find clothes for fantasy you, as Ralph deals in all sorts of fantasies. He can transform you into a Park Avenue princess, a prairie settler, a downhill racer—whomever you want to be, chances are Ralph has what you need to get there. He doesn't mess around.

The pants are pretty cool leather pants, but it's the fringe on the side that really brings the fantasy to life. Very few professions aside from rock star embrace fringe. So when you put on these pants, you can instantly imagine yourself onstage—it wouldn't be a stretch if you found yourself telling people you once opened for Tom Petty.

These pants were expensive, and I've only worn them once, so that's my main regret. I don't feel a need to wear them out in public, but I should wear them more at home. If Tina Turner could be a private dancer, I could be a private rock star.

Kyle Hotchkiss Carone *Restaurateur/partner at Cafe Clover, New York City*

REGRETTABLE ARTICLE OF CLOTHING: Paisley sweater

PURCHASED: Kenzo boutique, Paris, in 2012, for $600

TIMES WORN: 5 or 6

I was visiting Paris for a few days during fashion week. Somehow, a few days turned into a week, and I ran out of clothes. I guess I could have done laundry, but doing laundry in French seemed like a lot of effort and going shopping was more fun.

This sweater is much better from a distance. Up close, it's sort of an odd dance of micro-paisleys that look they were made on a fancy Spirograph. I've found it's good to wear to a meeting when you want to come off as a touch eccentric. "Why is this guy not wearing a coat and tie, and what's the deal behind that sweater?"

I've also worn the sweater to family get-togethers. You always have to give family fresh ammunition for ridicule. I consider this sweater a gift to them.

Krissy Jones *Yoga teacher, New York City*

REGRETTABLE ARTICLE OF CLOTHING: Ivy sweat suit

PURCHASED: PegLegNYC.com, in 2015, for $350

TIMES WORN: 1

This outfit had a lot of good things going for it. My boyfriend designed it, so I could be a supportive girlfriend by wearing it. I got it at a huge discount because of said boyfriend. It also fit really well and was easy to put on and take off, big pluses for a yoga teacher. But no matter how hard I tried to convince myself, it just didn't work for me.

Maybe a single piece of ivy-themed workout gear would be OK, but the pants and top together look like something a health-conscious Batman villain would wear.

I wore it to work one day and decided to count how many people stared at me (and not in a good way) on my commute. I made a deal with myself that if more than two people stared, I wouldn't wear the ivy combo again. This was in New York City, where people have seen everything, and I still counted four people who stared. Four people in New York equals twenty-six people in Cincinnati or St. Louis, so that settled it. I was officially dropping out of the ivy league.

It looks like something a health-conscious Batman villain would wear.

James Shepherd *College student, Stonington, Connecticut*

REGRETTABLE ARTICLE OF CLOTHING: Denim jacket

PURCHASED: Haight Street, San Francisco, in November 2012, for $5

TIMES WORN: 25

Since I bought this jacket at a thrift shop, I often wonder about who owned it before me. On the back of the jacket it reads, *World Roller Derby Alliance*, so it possibly was once owned by someone named "The Sadistic Slammer" or "The Bone Crusher."

I've Googled *World Roller Derby Alliance* a few times with little success. I imagined the jacket could have been given away at some international Roller Derby conference, when all the Roller Derby teams from around the globe converge. However, there's probably a greater likelihood that it was just a phrase that some company in China slapped on the back to sell jackets.

I don't know a lot about Roller Derby, but every time I wear the jacket my room-mate, Quinton, likes to point out that Roller Derby is a very popular women's sport, so I'm probably wearing some lady's jacket. I think I'm OK with that.

Billy Richards *Musician, New York City*

REGRETTABLE ARTICLE OF CLOTHING: Crocodile-skin biker jacket

PURCHASED: New York, in 2014, for $1,000

TIMES WORN: 20

This jacket makes me nervous. Not because I don't like it, but because I'm constantly worried something bad will happen to it. The jacket is genuine crocodile and was made by a friend who hunts and tans the crocodiles in addition to designing clothing. The jacket would be crazy expensive if my friend didn't give me a deal, so every time I wear it, I'm a little on guard that I'll lose it or be mugged for it. I see myself ending up as a *New York Post* headline: "Man Killed During Croc Coat Caper!"

One night, I wore the jacket to a club that had the heat turned up so high, you could have raised orchids in there. I wanted to take off the jacket, but there was no way I was going to trust the coat check. I lost about five pounds that night.

I've never owned an article of clothing that puts me on edge. Before I leave the house, I debate whether I want to spend the evening worrying about the jacket. Yes, it's cool and I'll get compliments, but should a jacket really make you want to take a Xanax? I don't think so.

Should a jacket make you want to take Xanax?

Lara Speier *App designer, New York City*

REGRETTABLE ARTICLE OF CLOTHING: Baroque coat

PURCHASED: Palm Beach, Florida, in 2013, for $85

TIMES WORN: 1

When you go shopping with your mom, you're apt to buy things you wouldn't normally buy. It's not just because she's paying, it's also because she's your mother, and she has some inexplicable hold over you that enables her to convince you of things that no other human can.

We were in Palm Beach (of course) when my mother spotted the coat in a consignment store. She instantly began listing places where I could wear it and possible ways it could be accessorized. "To the theater with a pencil skirt and some cute flats"; "to lunch with a pair of black leather pants." She was imagining my life as the Anne Hathaway montage scene in *Devil Wears Prada*, except for that jaunty newsboy cap and really annoying friends.

The jacket is way too big for me, and the puffy sleeves take it into costume territory. It's very Mozart-goes-clubbing, so in order to wear it, I'd have to have it rebuilt by a tailor at considerable expense. This puts it on my list of things I say I'll do but probably never will, along with moving to Barcelona and learning how to drive a stick shift.

Sometimes when my mom calls, she'll ask about the coat. I guarantee her that I still have it, and we inevitably start to talk about our trip to Palm Beach and say we should plan another trip and try to see each other more. Hmm, I'm beginning to realize my mom is a very clever lady.

143

Douglas Hand *Attorney for fashion and lifestyle brands,*

New York City and Los Angeles

REGRETTABLE ARTICLE OF CLOTHING: Steven Alan suit

PURCHASED: New York City, in 2013

TIMES WORN: 4

The relationship you have with your clothes is sort of like dating. You take an item out a few times and see how it feels. Sometimes it works and the relationship takes off; other times, you quickly learn you weren't made for each other and go your separate ways. That was the case with this suit. If this suit had been a person, it was definitely a time when I would have had to say, "The problem is *me*, not *you*."

The suit is a perfectly fine suit. On the right person, it would look great. I am not that person. The suit is cut a bit narrow, with extra-slim lapels and a short jacket, and it's made from a shiny fabric that is body-hugging. I'm secretly a big guy, so on me it looks like I stole a bellhop uniform from some twee hotel. If I had one of those little round hats with a chin strap, you could drop me into almost any Wes Anderson movie.

I wore the suit to the office a few times, but I found myself being a little self-conscious and needing to explain it to people. Again, it was sort of like running into friends when you're on a bad date. Do you really have to introduce everyone when you know they're never going to see one another again?

The suit and I amicably parted ways. And I'm confident there is someone out there who will love it. I think we both knew it wasn't going to work. I just hope that down the road, the suit doesn't show up at my door drunk, ringing my buzzer at 3:00 a.m.

144

It looks like I stole a bellhop uniform from some twee hotel.

Ira Silverberg *Book editor, New York City and Bellport, NY*

REGRETTABLE ARTICLE OF CLOTHING: Hermès smoking jacket

PURCHASED: Hermès sample sale, in the summer of 1998, for $500

TIMES WORN: 1

Sample sales make you do crazy things. Items you would normally never buy become must-haves when their prices have been chopped more times than Lizzie Borden's parents. Sample sales result in your closet and home being cluttered with things that you will never use or wear. But you do get a rush every time you force people to guess how little you paid for these unnecessary items. "Sure, I'll never use it, but can you believe how cheap it was?"

The Hermès sale is the king of all sample sales. Everything is extravagant, luxurious, and totally impractical. Imagine if Baron Munchausen had a garage sale. Here, you'll find fuchsia cashmere blankets trimmed in ermine, genuine alligator shoehorns, and saddles converted to wastebaskets. It is also where I found my smoking jacket.

I threw a New Year's Eve dinner to celebrate the new year but also to give myself an opportunity to wear my new jacket. I converted my office space into a glamorous salon. I rented round tables and ballroom chairs and had elaborate flower arrangements everywhere. It really was gorgeous, although the large copy machine was a little hard to disguise, even under a tablecloth. The smoking jacket was the perfect thing to wear that night, but once you've worn it, you've worn it.

I've always wondered if designers create certain items they know will never sell at retail just because they're fun to make. I imagine some little man in France holding up my smoking jacket, proud of his creation and quietly whispering, "Zee zample zale."

Divya Anantharaman *Taxidermist, Brooklyn*

REGRETTABLE ARTICLE OF CLOTHING: Lolita dress

PURCHASED: London, in 2005, for $50

TIMES WORN: 8

You might need a little background to understand this dress and why I bought it. Because this isn't just a dress, it's a movement.

In Japan, there is a whole subculture of girls and guys who dress in a style known as Lolita. It's a combination of Victorian style and Goth with a dash of Scarlett O'Hara. There are entire neighborhoods where everyone dresses like this. It's a thing.

I was living in London when Lolita style came thundering in. I had a lot more free time back then, so I could spend my days planning my outfits, which is what any good Lolita-ite does.

I saw the dress in a store window and walked by it every day until I had saved up enough money to buy it. Then the fun began. I would create different characters using the dress, accessories, makeup, hairstyles, props, or whatever I could find. A birdcage, a paper fan, old doll parts—all these items might make their way into my daily look. The more outrageous, the better. People commented that I looked like something out of a Tim Burton movie, so I knew my Lolita game must be strong.

My dress-up days are behind me now, and my Lolita dress stays in the closet. But I do hope there's a girl somewhere in Tokyo right now carrying the Lolita torch, wearing five petticoats and trying to figure out how to turn a fondue pot into a hat.

Colin Stokes *Assistant cartoon editor at* The New Yorker, *London originally, currently Brooklyn*

REGRETTABLE ARTICLE OF CLOTHING: Teddy Boy drape jacket

PURCHASED: Hornets of Kensington, London, in 2008, for $120

TIMES WORN: 20

Some clothing should come with a warning label. Not the type you find on cheap Halloween costumes that casually mention you might spontaneously combust, but a label that lets the person buying it know there may be some social risks involved in wearing it. Basically, wear this and you will look like a complete wanker.

When I was living in London, I went to Hornets on a regular basis. Hornets is a particularly good secondhand men's store. It carries all the requisite items you'd find in a proper gentleman's closet: bespoke suits, handmade shoes, cricket jackets, riding boots. If Lord Grantham ended up on the skids and needed to unload his wardrobe for quick cash, this is where he would go.

During one visit, I found an original Teddy Boy jacket. Teddy Boys were guys in 1950s London who dressed like Edwardian dandies but who would also break a bottle over your head if they felt like it. They were badass fops. So of course I needed the jacket.

When I moved to New York and wore the jacket, it didn't seem to have the same cachet it did in London. In New York, I was mistaken for a bellhop and snickered at by a pack of little girls, and I terrified a college roommate who couldn't fathom why I would seriously wear "that weird Michael Jackson coat" on the street.

I was snickered at by a pack of little girls.

Isel Garcia-Renart *Burlesque dancer, Falmouth, Massachusetts*

REGRETTABLE ARTICLE OF CLOTHING: Daisy shirt

PURCHASED: Los Angeles, in 2010, for $10

TIMES WORN: 6

When I found this shirt in a $10-or-less bin at a store on Melrose, I felt I had majorly scored. I'm a girl who can't resist a bargain—or, apparently, a shirt with a peekaboo side cutout.

The shirt was lightweight, blousy, and breezy, so I decided to wear it as a beach cover-up. However, I failed to factor in the flower cutout on the side of the shirt. After a day in the sun, I discovered I had a daisy-shaped tan mark on my midriff that was about three shades darker than the rest of my skin. It looked like one of those rubber appliqués people put down in their bathtubs to keep from falling. It took a few days to fade, but if I went back out in the sun it would reappear.

Since the tanning incident, the shirt has become that last item I wear before I admit to myself that I really need to do laundry. I have a feeling its next stop is Goodwill. When I drop it off, I think I should include a note outlining the possible hazards of wearing it—I wish someone had warned me about possible side-daisy side effects.

Ingrid Carozzi *Florist/owner of Tin Can Studios, Brooklyn*

REGRETTABLE ARTICLE OF CLOTHING: Pluto sweatshirt

PURCHASED: Stockholm, in 1992, for $5

TIMES WORN: 8

Here are facts I've learned about two things named Pluto. One is no longer a planet, and the other was never really a star.

When I found this Pluto sweatshirt back in my hometown of Stockholm in the 1990s, I was really excited. I bought it at Myrorna, which sounds like a cool boutique but is actually the Swedish version of the Salvation Army. Clothes with cartoon characters on them were very popular in Sweden, especially American ones. At clubs you'd see shirts and jackets featuring Mickey Mouse, Betty Boop, and Woody Woodpecker, among others, but I doubt the people wearing them knew anything about the characters aside from the fact that they were popular in America. Sadly, I was soon to discover that a certain yellow dog was not the celebrity I assumed him to be.

When I arrived in America, I thought I'd see Pluto everywhere. When I didn't, I asked people about him. They'd mumble something about Disney and Pluto's murky relationship with Goofy, but couldn't tell me much more. They did clue me into the fact that Pluto was not terribly popular these days, if he ever was. A quick search on the Pluto Wiki page showed that he hadn't made a movie since the 1950s!

Pluto was no Bart Simpson—there was no Pluto breakfast cereal, no Pluto shampoo, nor would I be seeing a Pluto float in the Macy's Thanksgiving Day Parade. I was crushed to learn that all this time, I'd been wearing the sweatshirt of a has-been or, even worse, a never-was.

Carlos Huber _Creator of Arquiste Parfumeur, fragrance developer,_
New York City

REGRETTABLE ARTICLE OF CLOTHING: Embroidered vest

PURCHASED: Mérida, Mexico, in 2011, for $20

TIMES WORN: 1

I always like to bring back something from everywhere I travel. Mérida is a beautiful place, but it's not exactly a hot spot for arts and crafts like some other areas of Mexico. My choices were basically limited to place mats, sombreros, or this vest.

The vest is one of those things that looks a lot better off than on. It's a little boxy, and if you wear it alone, people will definitely assume you're either going to or have just been to some kind of festival. I've decided you need to wear the vest under a jacket so just a little bit of it peeks out like a surprise.

I've also considered framing the vest, but where would I hang it? OK, it's official: I have thought way too much about this vest.

157

This vest is one of those things that looks a lot better off than on.

Brad Fisher (and Freddy) *Model/artist, New York City*

REGRETTABLE ARTICLE OF CLOTHING: Budweiser blazer

PURCHASED: Thrift store, in 2005, for $7

TIMES WORN: 14

I've seen shorts, hats, and tube tops featuring the Budweiser label, but I've never seen another blazer. I like to think it's a highly coveted jacket in the beer industry, commissioned by the brewery and bestowed upon only the most successful beer distributors. Maybe it's like the green jackets they give away at The Masters—a coat of honor.

I got the jacket at a thrift store but then had it altered at a tailor. The alterations cost about twenty times what I paid for the jacket. I believe if you're going to have one alcohol-themed article of clothing, it should fit properly.

The jacket only comes out once a year, on the Fourth of July. It's become somewhat of a tradition. Friends of mine know that when things start exploding in the sky, they'll see me in the jacket. I always get compliments, but the people doing the complimenting are usually drunk, so I'm not sure that counts.

Oh, and as for Freddy's Santa sweater, he hates it. He gets moody at the holidays.

158

Marianne Daly *Waitress/cranberry-farm worker, Cape Cod, Massachusetts*

REGRETTABLE ARTICLE OF CLOTHING: Carhartt coverall

PURCHASED: eBay, in 2008, for $22.97

TIMES WORN: 30

I like to think of this as my hibernation outfit. It's what I wear when I want to go into a cocoon state. I initially bought the coverall to wear when working in the cranberry bogs, but I soon discovered that they also allowed me to be a bit incognito when I felt like it. It's rather fun sometimes to just zip them up, stroll past people you know, and seem invisible. I usually pair them with an Elmer Fudd–type hat with flaps, which greatly helps with my stealth maneuvers.

The only regret I have about buying the coverall is that I didn't buy any extras. Who knew that coveralls would skyrocket in price? Lesson learned—always buy in bulk.

161

Patrick Grant *Savile Row guv'nor/designer and owner at E. Tautz*

and Norton & Sons/host of The Great British Sewing Bee, *London*

REGRETTABLE ARTICLE OF CLOTHING: Tartan bomber jacket

PURCHASED: Edinburgh, Scotland, in 1986, for about $2

TIMES WORN: 1

Long before I landed on Savile Row, I was a boy in Edinburgh who had a love of clothes and no money. So many hours were spent at Flip of Hollywood, a giant secondhand shop that sadly is no longer there. It was an incredible place, with racks and racks of everything imaginable, including probably fleas.

The jacket was bought as somewhat of an homage to the Bay City Rollers, a boy band from Scotland at the time that was famous for tartan clothes and feathered hair. Though at eighteen, I may not have known the word *homage*.

I tried on the jacket countless times in front of the mirror, but it never actually made it out of the house. The fact that I've held onto it all these years must say something, but what that is, I'm not exactly sure.

Chloe King *Digital PR and social media manager for Bergdorf Goodman, New York City*

REGRETTABLE ARTICLE OF CLOTHING: Party dress

PURCHASED: New York City, in 2013, $400

TIMES WORN: 1

I recently heard one of the Real Housewives going on about how royal blue was "her color." All of the Real Housewives seem to run together for me in a blonde blur, so I'm not sure which one she was, but what she said is something you hear a lot of people say: that a certain color is "their color." Some colors, I've learned, are nobody's color.

I was with some friends at a sample sale when I spotted the dress. When I first saw it, I had a visceral reaction, but I wasn't sure if it was a good reaction or a bad reaction. Did I love this dress or hate it? My friends decided I loved it. (Thanks, friends!) We then had a discussion as to what color it was: "apple-martini green"; "chartreuse"; "if a lemon and a lime had a baby." We finally settled on "acid green," and I bought the dress.

Here's a tip: If you want to get out of something or fake sick, just put on an acid green dress. People will instantly ask if you're feeling OK because your skin takes on a strange gray-green glow.

Some colors are your friend. Navy blue and pale pink, sure, you could invite them to lunch and they'd be charming and not have a bad word to say about anyone. Acid green should never be on your guest list. Acid green is nobody's friend. Acid green is nobody's color.

We had a discussion about what color this dress was: "apple-martini green"; "chartreuse"; "if lemon and lime had a baby."

Christina Caradona *Model/fashion blogger at Trop Rouge,*

New York City

REGRETTABLE ARTICLE OF CLOTHING: Dress

PURCHASED: Vintage store, New York City, in 2012, for $100

TIMES WORN: 10

Just as there are jogging shoes and smoking jackets, I like to think of this as my drinking dress. For some reason, whenever I'm at home having a couple of cocktails, I like to put it on. It's almost Pavlovian—I see a corkscrew and instantly feel a need to wear it. The dress is really comfortable, and if by chance red wine or a margarita were spilled on it, I wouldn't mind. It might even give it more character.

The dress is an indoor dress, too. Sort of like those house cats that get declawed, it never gets to play outside. I like to wear it within the confines of my own home, turn up the music really loud, and dance wildly. It puts me in touch with my inner hippie. If J.Crew ever created a Manson Family collection, I could definitely see this dress as part of it.

Like those house cats that get declawed, this dress never gets to play outside.

Katalina Hicks *Digital strategist, London*

REGRETTABLE ARTICLE OF CLOTHING: Herve Leger bandeau bandage dress

PURCHASED: Net-a-Porter, in 2003, for $800

TIMES WORN: 1

When someone dubs something "classy and elegant," chances are the thing itself and the person doing the dubbing are probably neither. Sadly, that is true in the case of this unfortunate little Herve Leger number.

I was dating a hedge funder person at the time—he was the dubber—and we were going to the opening of the infamous Marquee nightclub, which bills itself as the "quintessential ultra-lounge" (that just about says it all). This was at the start of the millennium and the height of conspicuous consumption, when people lived for a sighting of Leo or Paris at the next table and lit Cohibas with $100 bills. OK, I never actually saw this done, but it was in a movie so it must have happened. I wanted to wear something to the opening that was a little out of my comfort zone. I ended up wearing something that was a little more in the Twilight Zone.

The dress is a style that's meant to resemble bandages. I'm not sure why or how it happened, but for a brief fashion moment, it was a thing. You were supposed to look like a hot mummy—and by mummy I mean sarcophagus dweller, not a British mother.

Despite the dress looking like it would hug my body, it proved to do just the opposite. It kept falling down throughout the evening, forcing me to have one hand on my chest at all times. Try doing that while holding a lit cigarette and a glass of Malbec!

Charles Graeber *Journalist/author of the* New York Times *best seller* The Good Nurse, *Brooklyn and Nantucket*

REGRETTABLE ARTICLE OF CLOTHING: Kimono

PURCHASED: Kyoto, Japan, in 2013, for $20

TIMES WORN: 15

You wear one little kimono, and suddenly everybody's Don Rickles. Here is a sampling of comments inspired by this kimono: "the samurai with a secret," "Jame Gumb," "Culture Club's last groupie," "Johnny Depp-sperate," "Geisha Goy," "Floral Henderson," "Fat Brando," "Robes Pierre," "Hello and Goodbye Kitty," "the Big Sleazy," "Flower Drum Wrong," "Housecoat Harry," "Liberace's pool boy," "the mayor of Key West," "Mrs. Roper," "Yoko Kimono," "Godzilla's stylist," and my personal favorite, "La Cage aux Fuckstick."

Stephanie Krasnoff *Owner of American Two Shot boutique, New York City*

REGRETTABLE ARTICLE OF CLOTHING: Matching vintage shirt and skirt

PURCHASED: Water Mill New York, in 2011, for about $250

TIMES WORN: 1

There are two schools of thought on this outfit, and neither of them is good.

One side says that I'm too old for this combo. When I bought it, I thought it seemed vaguely familiar. I discovered why when looking through family photos and saw myself in an almost identical outfit—when I was seven. I had flashbacks of wearing it with Mary Janes to birthday parties and riding ponies. So I'm thinking this look is too "junior," as they say, for me to pull off at this point in my life. Once you can vote and have a gynecologist, you probably shouldn't be wearing matchy-matchy flowered sets.

However, on the other hand, am I too young to wear this outfit? If you go to Boca or any other town that is populated by ladies of a certain age who enjoy the early-bird special and playing canasta, you see a fair amount of outfits that look like this. Until I start looking forward to a *Matlock* marathon, I don't think I should be wearing this ensemble.

172

I had flashbacks of wearing it with Mary Janes to birthday parties.

Jesse Israel *Entrepreneur, Brooklyn and Los Angeles*

REGRETTABLE ARTICLE OF CLOTHING: Puma tie-dye jacket

PURCHASED: New York City, in 2013, for $100

TIMES WORN: 1

I'm generally a fan of tie-dye. I like the whole Deadhead world associated with it. But I like old-school tie-dye that you do yourself with rubber bands and white T-shirts and Rit dye that ruins your bathtub. Factory-generated tie-dye seems like cheating.

When I bought this jacket, I didn't realize it was faux tie-dye. I thought it looked more like Rorschach-test inkblots. I was looking forward to asking people what they saw in the patterns of my jacket. "A steak fajita, really? Hmm."

I do a lot of bike riding and thought, for some reason, that the jacket also had a reflective element to it. Wrong again. I could have sworn it did in the store, but when I got it home, it was just a basic jacket.

From this unfortunate purchase, I've learned I really need to pay more attention to what I'm buying. Otherwise I may end up with more clothes I don't like that could maybe get me run over.

175

Yearbook

176

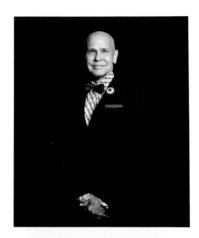

178

Mikey DeTemple
www.mikeydetemple.com
Twitter: @mikeydetemple
Instagram: @mikeydetemple

Annie Dewitt
www.talllikethreeapples.wordpress.com
Twitter: @talllike3apples

Angela Dimayuga
www.missionchinesefood.com
Instagram: @swimsuit_issue
Instagram: @missionchinesefood

Claire Distenfeld
www.fivestoryny.com
Twitter/Instagram: @FivestoryNY
Instagram: @claire_fivestory

Robby Doyle

Virginia Elwood
www.virginiaelwood.com
www.savedtattoo.com
Instagram: @virginiaelwood

Adam Green
www.adamgreen.net
www.adamgreensaladdin.com
Twitter: @averagecabbage
Instagram: @averagecabbage

Claire Griffin

Dennis Gronim
Twitter: @dgronim

Doug Hand
www.hballp.com
Twitter: @HandoftheLaw
Instagram: @handofthelaw

Matt Hanna
Twitter: @matthannanyc
Instagram: @matthanna19

Katalina Hicks
Instagram: @katahicks

183

184

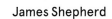

187

188

189

Tom Coleman (@snowmanz86) is an Emmy-nominated writer and filmmaker who has worked with MTV, *Esquire*, and *McSweeny's*. He can tie a bow tie without looking in the mirror and wishes he knew more about cheese. He lives in New York City.

Jerome Jakubiec is a fashion, portrait, and celebrity photographer whose work has been published in magazines worldwide. For more information, visit www.jeromejakubiec.com.

Special thanks to Vanessa Mobley for taking time out from working on serious books to guide us along with this one; our unflappable and thoughtful agent, Monika Verma; design Guru, Ahmer Kalam; and our editor at Rizzoli, Kathleen Jayes.

Thanks to Amy Corcoran and Charles Spiegal, Shrevie and Jim Shepherd, Mia and John Coveny, Liza Powel O'Brien, Joanie and Bob Hall, Connie Wilsterman, Mark Murray, Douglas Rogers, Ted McCagg, Geraldine Nager, Sarah Larson, Marc Porter, Jim Hennessy, Marianne Raphael, Adam Higginbotham, Paula Enstice, Maryjoan Eberhardt, Sean Wilsey, Mark Strong, Lisa Baker, Tom Cutler, Janet Currie, Anthony Enstice, Brent Stoller, Matt Giulvezan, Axel Dupeux, Emilio Nunez, Theo Blackston, Jules Hulburd, Andy Snyder, and all our family and friends who listened to us ramble on about this book for the past four years.

First published in the United States of America in 2017
by Rizzoli International Publications, Inc.
300 Park Avenue South
New York, NY 10010
www.rizzoliusa.com

Designed by MGMT. design

2017 2018 2019 2020 / 10 9 8 7 6 5 4 3 2 1

Distributed in the U.S. trade by Random House, New York

Printed in China

ISBN-13: 978-0-8478-5973-3

Library of Congress Catalog Control Number: 2016953381